But God

A Youth Devotional

by Katy Newton Naas

Published by HIS Books

This devotional is dedicated to my sons, Aven and Brayson. I pray you both use your "But God" moments to share incredible testimonies with the world someday!

I don't think there's a single person in this world who can look around at this world - this big, beautiful world - and not see how broken it really is.

We don't have to look at the other side of the world to see the mess we live in. We can look down our hallways at school. In our communities. In our own homes. We have an enemy who comes to "steal, kill, and destroy" (John 10:10), and he is running rampant everywhere we look.

But God.

We serve a God who is active in our lives. A God who steps in when things seem hopeless or impossible and transforms even the darkest situations. A God who is in control, a God whose plans will ultimately prevail even when we can't see a way out of whatever mess surrounds us.

All throughout the Bible, we see God working. Although He gives us free will, our God doesn't just sit back and watch the events unfold. He moves in situations and in hearts simply because He loves us.

Over and over again, we see God make a way when it doesn't seem remotely possible. A God who parts entire seas, a God who heals, a God who brings the dead back to life. A God of miracles.

In this devotional, we will look at some of the greatest "But God" moments from the Bible. We will get to know this God who is *still* moving, and working, and performing miracles; and we will study what it means to have a real, meaningful, life-changing relationship with Him.

Give God a little time each day. Get to know Him as our awesome, powerful, and almighty Creator...as well as our loving, merciful, and forgiving Father.

In Him, there is love. There is peace. And no matter your situation, there is hope. Always hope. Because even in your worst moments, He is there. And there is a "But God" story for your life, too.

Day 1: Noah

We might think this world we live in today is full of evil. And we would be right, of course. But evil is nothing new. Way back in the early days of the world, it didn't take long for men to corrupt the perfect world God created.

God's plan for humanity was falling apart. When God looked at the people who continued to multiply and fill the land, He saw nothing but wickedness. Their thoughts and intentions were evil. And on top of that, fallen angels who followed Satan began to take human women as wives, creating a race of giants called Nephilim.

God grieved for the evil He saw. He began to regret even creating man. Finally, He decided to do something drastic - He would destroy the world and start over.

The story of mankind could have ended right there.

BUT GOD.

There was one man - only one - who found favor in God's eyes. His name was Noah, and he was a righteous man who followed God. God went to Noah and told him of His plans to destroy the earth. He told Noah to build an ark out of gopher wood, giving him very specific instructions on the dimensions and number of rooms inside of it. Noah and his family would be the only survivors, along with two of every animal that would come to Noah in order to keep the species alive.

Let's be clear about a couple of things. First of all, Noah was over five hundred years old when God came to him with these instructions. He was not a builder, and wouldn't have had a clue where to begin when it came to following God's instructions. He didn't have power tools or a construction crew to help him. Building this ark was a HUGE task. Second, up to this point, *it had never rained before*. Plants and trees received the water they needed from the ground. No one had ever seen rain fall from the sky, and the idea that the world would flood seemed insane.

But Noah's faith was bigger than any doubts. He took on the task, building the ark with his family, even when the people around him thought he had lost his mind. And just as God told him, the animals came to him in pairs. Noah and his family went into the ark when Noah was six hundred years old, and for the first time ever, rain began to fall.

Rain fell for forty days and nights before it stopped, but the waters stayed for months. Noah and his family lived in the ark, waiting patiently until the waters finally began to subside. Finally, Noah saw dry ground when he landed the ark at the top of a mountain. He and his family, along with the animals, finally left the ark and started over.

God blessed Noah and his sons. He made a covenant with them that he would never again flood the whole world, putting his rainbow in the sky as a sign of that covenant.

Verse to Remember - Genesis 9:16
Find this verse in your Bible and write it below.

____

____

____

____

Reflect - What if Noah would have refused to listen to God? What if he had been too ashamed to do something that seemed "crazy" to the world? If Noah had chosen not to believe God, you wouldn't be here right now, reading this devotional.

Sometimes following God and doing what's right in his eyes will be deemed crazy to the outside world. Sometimes God will whisper an idea in your heart that may seem "out there" at first. Choose to trust Him anyway! Remember God's plan is always better, and His ways are always higher. Write a prayer below, asking God to help you say yes to Him and have faith in Him no matter the situation. Ask Him to help you follow His word, even when you're doing it alone.

____

____

____

____

____

____

____

____

Day 2: Job

The story of Job is unique in that it allows us to see interaction between God and Satan, something we don't get a firsthand account of often in the Bible. It starts off with a description of Job, calling him "blameless and upright, one who feared God and turned away from evil" (Job 1:1). Right away, we get a picture of a good man who was very blessed by God - he had hundreds of animals, many servants, and ten children. Job prayed often and even prayed on behalf of his children, just in case they did something wrong.

After learning a little about Job, the scene changes to heaven, where Satan comes to see God. They have a conversation about Job, and Satan says the only reason Job is so faithful to God is because God has given him so much and protects him. He says that if Job loses what God has given him, he will curse God. So, the Lord gives Satan permission to take away the blessings he has given Job.

This can be hard to wrap our minds around. Satan is allowed to talk to God in heaven? Apparently so. God allows Satan to do harm? He does. Keep in mind, God gives us all free will. He doesn't force anyone to do the "right thing" or to follow him; we are all given a mind of our own and can make our own choices. When Satan causes harm, God can and does intervene at times. Other times, he allows the evil to happen. That's hard to grasp. But one thing we can take comfort in is this: God will work things together for our good. He can use even the worst situations, the worst evil, and bring good from it. Romans 8:28 promises us that if we love Him, He will work all things together for our good. Ultimately, he would do so for Job, too.

But before He could work His plan, Satan started throwing the hits at Job. In the course of one day, Job lost his animals, his servants, and his children. He tore his robe and shaved his head - common signs of mourning in that day - but then he did something amazing: he fell down in worship. He recognized God as the God who gives and takes away, and decided to praise Him through it all.

But Satan wasn't done. When he saw that Job was still faithful to God, he attacked again, this time going after Job's health. He struck him with sores that covered his body from head to toe. Even Job's wife encouraged Job to curse God at this point, but Job still remained faithful. He pointed out that if we receive good from God, we can receive the bad, too. Job's friends came to be with him, trying to offer comfort, but basically accused him of some hidden sin that caused these horrible things to happen to him. All the while, Job maintained his innocence, crying out to God.

BUT GOD.

Finally, God answered. He reminded Job just who He is: the Creator of everything and the Provider for all. He reminded Job that He is all-knowing and can be trusted. Then, He did something amazing: He restored all that Job had, but twice as much. He ended up having ten more children and went on to live a full life, seeing four generations of children after his own.

It's hard to understand why evil is allowed to happen, and it's okay to talk to God and even question what's happening when you're in a situation that's difficult or painful. But remember Job and how God brought joy and blessings back to his life again, and know that He's always working on your behalf, too.

Verse to Remember - Job 1:21
Find this verse in your Bible and write it below.

____

____

____

____

Reflect - For some reason, it's easy to forget just how big our God really is. When you need a reminder, read Revelation 4. This is a vision John had of God on His throne in heaven. Some of the imagery is difficult to even picture, but if you really read it slowly and try to take it in, you will get a small idea of how mighty and powerful He is, and how beautiful heaven will be one day.

Read Revelation 4. In the space below, write about the parts that stood out to you most. Why did those images stand out to you? How does it help you imagine just how incredible it will be to see Him on His throne in heaven someday?

____

____

____

____

____

____

____

Day 3: Abraham

Abraham, or Abram as he was originally called, was chosen by God to be the father of the Israelite people. Though Abraham was 75 years old and he and his wife Sarah (previously known as Sarai) didn't have any children, God promised Abraham he would become a great nation. He promised to bless him and his family, and told him that all the families of earth would be blessed through him (which came true, because Jesus came from the line of Abraham's descendants).

To receive these blessings, Abraham had to follow God's plan for his life. This plan included leaving behind his home country and his family to go to the land God had in store for him. Abraham obeyed…sort of. He took his wife with him, which was great, but he also took his nephew even though God told him to leave his family behind. Despite this, God blessed him. When they went to Egypt, Pharaoh was taken by Sarah's beauty and wanted to marry her. God protected Abraham by sending plagues upon Pharaoh until they released Sarah and let them continue on their journey.

When they reached the land where God intended them to settle, God reminded Abraham of His promise: "Look toward heaven, and number the stars, if you are able to number them…So shall your offspring be" (Genesis 15:5). At this point, Abraham and Sarah still didn't have any children, but again, Abraham believed what God said.

Like many of us do, Abraham and Sarah began to get impatient. They thought they would "help" God's plan by speeding things up. In a culture where it was common to have more than one wife, Sarah encouraged Abraham to marry their servant, Hagar, to let her have a child for them. The plan worked…but it was never God's plan, and Abraham and Sarah quickly figured out that when you try to do things your own way, things never go the way you hope they will. It didn't take long before Sarah grew jealous of Hagar and began mistreating her and her son. It eventually got so bad that Abraham had to send them away. But despite the fact that once again, Abraham had failed to fully obey God, God was still faithful. When Abraham was ninety-nine years old, God promised him yet again that Sarah was going to have a baby.

When Sarah heard the news, she laughed.

BUT GOD.

Soon enough, Sarah gave birth to a son named Isaac. Through Isaac's line, the Israelite people grew and prospered. And through the long journey God led Abraham and Sarah through, they became great heroes of faith.

Verse to Remember - Genesis 12:2
Find this verse in your Bible and write it below.

____

____

____

____

Reflect - From the time God originally promised Abraham he would make him into a great nation until the time Sarah actually had Isaac, twenty-five years passed! That's a long time to wait for a promise to happen. No wonder Abraham and Sarah were tempted to take matters into their own hands...but look what happened when they did. They would have been better off to simply trust God and wait.

Over and over again in the Bible, through stories like these, we are reminded that God's timing is not like ours. We are impatient people and live in a culture when we want things to happen now, which makes it hard to wait.

On the lines below, write a prayer simply asking for patience. Ask God to help you trust His timing and to wait for His plans instead of trying to force things to happen on your own.

____

____

____

____

____

____

____

____

Day 4: Leah

Abraham's son, Isaac, married and had twin boys, Jacob and Esau. Jacob was the younger of the two and according to tradition, the older sibling is the one to receive the father's blessing. However, Jacob took advantage of Isaac's failing eyesight in his later years and tricked his father into blessing him instead of Esau. Esau was so furious, Jacob's life was in danger. He had to leave. His mother and father sent him to some distant family so he could find a wife.

Jacob fell in love with a woman named Rachel right away. Rachel had an older sister, Leah, but Rachel was the one Jacob was determined to marry. The Bible says "Leah's eyes were weak, but Rachel was beautiful in form and appearance" (Genesis 29:17). He made a deal with the girls' father that he would work for him for seven years in order to win her hand.

When the seven years were up, Jacob was prepared to take his wife. But their father played a trick of his own: he sent Leah in to be with Jacob.

The next morning, Jacob realized what had happened and erupted in rage. The father said he had to give his older daughter away first, and if he wanted Rachel, he could have her, too…for another seven years of service. Jacob agreed and worked seven more years so he could have the one he really wanted as his wife.

Jacob and Rachel are typically seen as the main characters in this story, but for this devotion, we are going to focus on the overlooked one: Leah. Leah was the innocent party in all of this, stuck with a husband who didn't love her and didn't want to be married to her. She wasn't beautiful like her sister and must have felt like she didn't have anything to offer to her husband.

BUT GOD.

God saw Leah's pain. Maybe Jacob didn't love her, but God did. He had a plan for her and gave her his favor, even when no one else in her life did. He blessed her through it: she was able to bear six sons and one daughter. Her sons would go on to form a big part of the twelve tribes of Israel, and her son Judah's line would include King David and even Jesus!

Though life wasn't easy for Leah, she trusted God. She praised Him for His blessings, focusing on the good in her life. Leah had no way of realizing that her descendants would include the Messiah, but she trusted that God was bringing something amazing out of her story. And He did!

Verse to Remember - Genesis 29:35
Find this verse in your Bible and write it below.

Reflect - God sees the entire picture, while we can only see bits and pieces of it. There will be times in your life when God is working and you can't see it. Maybe the blessings will come in your lifetime, or maybe they will come somewhere down the line. Regardless, you can be sure God always has a plan, and His plan is always good.

Write a prayer below, asking God to use even the difficult parts of your story for His good. Maybe you are going through difficult circumstances now. Maybe you are seeing bits and pieces of what's happening and want to see the big picture God sees. Think about Leah's story, and remember God can bring good out of anything. Ask Him to help you trust that He is working when it's hard to see His hand in everything.

Day 5: Joseph

Joseph was one of twelve brothers. He came from a troubled family - his dad, Jacob, had multiple wives…and one of them (Rachel) was the clear favorite. When Rachel had Joseph, he automatically became the favorite son, which caused a *lot* of jealousy with his brothers. When Jacob gave Joseph a special robe that showed his privilege, that jealousy deepened to hatred.

Joseph's dreams didn't help. He dreamed of his brothers' sheaves bowing down to his own. Then he dreamed of the sun, moon, and eleven stars bowing down to him. His brothers knew what both those dreams symbolized, and they hated the idea of ever bowing down to Joseph.

And one day, that hatred took over. When Joseph approached from a distance, they made a plan: they would kill Joseph and throw him into a pit, claiming an animal ate him. After the coaxing of one brother, they decided not to murder him, but to sell him as a slave to the Ishmaelites. This way, they would get rid of him and even make some money doing it! They took that special robe and dipped it in blood, which they gave to Jacob when they told him Joseph was devoured by a wild animal.

Put yourself in Joseph's position. Your brothers have ganged up on you and attacked, selling you off as a slave. The Ishmaelites sold him in Egypt to Potiphar, an officer of Pharaoh. He had to be scared. Lonely. He must have thought he would never see his family or his home again.

BUT GOD.

God's plan will always prevail, no matter how evil tries to thwart it.

Joseph became high-ranking in the house of Potiphar. He learned the language and customs and became well-respected. God was still working, still moving in Joseph's life. He used the evil the brothers committed for His plan.

Joseph hit some bumps and faced some mountains in Egypt. When Potiphar's wife tried to seduce him and he didn't have any part of it, she wrongfully accused him and he ended up in jail. Again, he must have felt terrified. Alone. Rejected.

But again…BUT GOD.

He rose up to gain favor, even in prison. And it was there in prison that he accurately interpreted dreams for two other prisoners, which ultimately led to the chance to interpret Pharaoh's dreams. And because he interpreted Pharaoh's dreams, he found himself basically second in command to the Pharaoh!

And even more importantly, he was able to save the country and all the others around Egypt when a famine plagued the land.

The craziest part for some people is that when his brothers showed up, hungry and desperate for food, he didn't turn them away in anger. He didn't scold them, or reject them, or tell them to get lost. When he revealed himself to them, he *forgave* them. He didn't pretend their sin never happened, but he offered grace and mercy they didn't deserve.

Verse to remember - Genesis 50:20
Find this verse in your Bible and write it below.

____

____

____

____

Reflect - Could you have been as forgiving as Joseph was in this situation? His brothers certainly didn't deserve his forgiveness - at least not by the world's standards - but Joseph gave it to them anyway.

Write a prayer below asking God to help you offer forgiveness to those in your life who hurt you or wrong you in some way. Ask Him to use even those bad moments for your good, as He did in the life of Joseph.

____

____

____

____

____

____

____

____

Day 6: Moses

Moses was born during a troubling time for the Hebrew people. They were enslaved in Egypt, where Pharaoh feared their growing population and decided to do something about it. He ordered the killing of all Hebrew baby boys because he felt it would weaken them and help him keep control. Moses was to be killed before he even had a chance to live.

BUT GOD.

Moses's mother defied the command, hiding Moses for three months before taking a leap of faith and sending him down the Nile River in a basket. This, too, could have led to his death, of course. So many things could have gone wrong on that river.

BUT GOD.

Moses was found…by Pharaoh's daughter, of all people. She took pity on him and decided to raise him in the Egyptian court. However, Moses grew up to resent the Egyptians who mistreated the Hebrew people. When he witnessed one taskmaster beating a Hebrew slave, he was filled with anger and murdered the Egyptian. When Pharaoh heard about the incident, he was ready to kill Moses.

BUT GOD.

Moses fled Egypt and ran to Midian. He lived a quiet life there, until God appeared to him in a burning bush. He told Moses he would be the one to deliver the Hebrew people from Egypt and lead them into the Promised Land. Moses wasn't sure he was up to the task - he wasn't confident in his speaking abilities - but God assured him that he and his brother Aaron were the ones for the job.

Moses confronted Pharaoh. He asked for the release of his people in the name of God, and Pharaoh refused. God sent a series of plagues upon the Egyptians, and finally, Pharaoh agreed to let them go. But they were barely even on their way before Pharaoh changed his mind and sent his army after them.

When they reached the Red Sea, Moses and the Hebrew people were trapped. The army was approaching on one side, and a giant sea was on the other. They had nowhere to run. They must have felt so hopeless.

BUT GOD.

God parted the waters of that sea, which allowed the Hebrew people to pass. The Egyptians, who ran in after them, were drowned when the waters closed again.

Time and time again, Moses's situation looked hopeless. And time and time again, God intervened and made a way when it seemed there was no way.

Verse to remember - Exodus 14:14
Find this verse in your Bible and write it below.

____

____

____

____

Reflect - Moses wasn't confident in his speaking abilities. Evidence even suggests that he had some sort of speech impediment. He tried to get out of what God wanted him to do...yet, when he finally said 'yes' to God, God used him to do incredible things.

In what areas of your life do you feel less than confident? What holds you back from being bold for God? Turn those things over to Him. Write a prayer to Him below, giving him the things you feel self-conscious about, and ask Him to use you for His plan however He wants to.

____

____

____

____

____

____

____

____

Day 7: Joshua

After Moses passed away, God chose Joshua to be the leader of the Israelites who would bring them into the Promised Land. "Now therefore arise, go over this Jordan, you and all this people, into the land that I am giving to them, to the people of Israel. Every place that the sole of your foot will tread upon I have given to you, just as I promised to Moses" (Joshua 1:2-3). God promised to be with Joshua in all he did and told him not to be afraid of what was to come. He assured Joshua, "No man shall be able to stand before you all the days of your life. Just as I was with Moses, so I will be with you" (Joshua 1:5). But for the Israelites to take over the land of Canaan, they had to win it piece by piece from the inhabitants who lived there.

They started with the city of Jericho, hoping to make it their first conquest. It wouldn't be easy; the city was protected with great walls.

BUT GOD.

Joshua sent spies who snuck into the walled city and hid, creating their plans to take over the city. God gave Joshua some strange instructions: he was to have his army march around the city once a day for six straight days. While marching, the priests carried the Ark of the Covenant while soldiers played their trumpets.

On the seventh day, the Israelites marched around those walls seven times. Joshua said to them, "Shout, for the LORD has given you the city. And the city and all that is within it shall be devoted to the LORD for destruction" (Joshua 6:16-17). With that, the men produced a powerful roar and watched as Jericho's walls miraculously fell down. The Israelite army was able to race in quickly and conquer the city.

Verse to Remember - Joshua 1:9
Find this verse in your Bible and write it below.

____

____

____

____

Reflect - Over and over again, we see God fulfill His promises. He often does it in unusual ways, as He did with the Battle of Jericho. It can be difficult to trust God to lead us over obstacles when we don't see how His plan will work, but stories like these help us see how important it is to rely on God and obey His commands, even when they don't seem to make sense.

Write a prayer below asking God to help you follow Him, even when the journey seems impossible or unexpected.

Day 8: Rahab

When Joshua sent those spies into Jericho, something amazing happened. The men were supposed to check out the city, but the walls around it protected it from outsiders. They came to the house of a woman named Rahab. Rahab wasn't a follower of God. In fact, she was known for living a life of sin.

BUT GOD.

Rahab believed in their God and wanted to help the men.

When the king heard the men were there, he sent men to Rahab's house who asked her to bring the Israelite men out. But Rahab protected them. She hid them on the roof in stalks of flax and said, "True, the men came to me, but I did not know where they were from. And when the gate was about to be closed at dark, the men went out. I do not know where the men went," (Joshua 2:4-5). The men sent by the king took off after them, hoping to catch them outside the city.

When they were gone, Rahab came to the roof where the men lay. She told the men she had heard about what God had done for them when He parted the Red Sea. She said that her people had great fear in their hearts because of the Israelites. "The LORD your God, He is God in the heavens above and on the earth beneath," she proclaimed (Joshua 2:11). She asked the men to remember her and her family when they took over the city, to spare their lives and treat them kindly. The men promised they would.

Rahab let them down using a rope through the window. She gave them advice for where to go in the hills in order to escape the men who pursued them. The men told her to gather her whole family into her house and tie a cord in the window where she had let them down. This would be a symbol to all the Israelite army to leave her house alone as they conquered the city.

Days later, the siege of Jericho succeeded. Just as the men promised, they conquered the entire city, but spared Rahab and her family.

Verse to Remember - Psalm 86:5
Find this verse in your Bible and write it below.

____

____

____

____

Reflect - Rahab played a huge role in helping the Israelites get the victory over Jericho. Despite her past, when she put her belief in God, He used her as a big part of His plan. In fact, she is even listed in the genealogy of Jesus! This woman with a sinful past ended up being an ancestor of Jesus.

This story is an awesome reminder that our past sin doesn't determine our future. You may have things you've done that you're not proud of, things you think might keep you from ever truly being part of God's plan. Or maybe you look around you at the "worst" sinners and assume there is no hope for them. Either way, when you remember Rahab and the plan God had for her, you can be sure no one is ever too far gone.

Write a prayer below, asking God to help you see yourself and others through His eyes. Ask Him to use you, despite your past failures. Ask Him to help you remember that He loves everyone and not to give up on the people around you who have chosen to live in sin.

____

____

____

____

____

____

____

____

Day 9: Gideon

There's a pattern throughout the Bible, where the Israelites go astray from God and start worshipping other gods. And every time, God removes His hand of protection from them, allowing them to be conquered by neighboring nations, until they repent of their sin and turn back to God once again.

The story of Gideon happened during one of those times. The Israelites had been straying from God for years before God allowed them to fall to the Midianites. Midian was so oppressive, stealing their crops and destroying their livestock.

In desperation, the Israelites cried out to God for help. God sent a prophet to them who reminded them how God had delivered them from slavery and from oppression, and yet they forgot all that so quickly and turned their backs on Him.

An angel appeared to a man named Gideon who was threshing wheat in a winepress, hoping to keep it from the Midianites. He told Gideon he was to be the one to lead the Israelite army to strike down the Midianites. He told Gideon to destroy the altar the people had made to Baal and use the wood from it to offer a sacrifice to the Lord.

Gideon was scared. He asked God to show him signs that he would be successful, and over and over again, God showed him the signs just like he asked.

Finally, Gideon did what God told him to do, but he took servants to help him complete the task at night because he was afraid of the townspeople and even his own family. And when the people woke up in the morning and saw Baal's altar demolished, they were furious.

Word got out that Gideon was responsible, and the people were prepared to kill him right then and there.

BUT GOD.

Gideon's father was able to calm the people by assuring them that Baal - if he was real - would deal with Gideon himself. The people accepted this and decided to leave Gideon alone.

Gideon gathered an army to go up against Midian. But God told Gideon he had too many men, and He didn't want the Israelites to think they had defeated the Midianites in their own strength.

Gideon offered the men who felt afraid the chance to leave. 22,000 men took him up on the offer, leaving 10,000.

But God said there were still too many. He had Gideon take the men to the water to get a drink and told him to separate the men based on the way they drank: the ones who kneeled down on their knees to drink were dismissed, but the ones who cupped their hands and lapped up the water were kept. Based on this system, only 300 men remained.

300 men didn't stand a chance against the tens of thousands of Midian soldiers.

BUT GOD.

During the night, God told Gideon to go against the enemy camp, because He was giving it into Gideon's hands. When Gideon arrived, the enemy seemed "like locusts in abundance" (Judges 7:12). But when he heard a man telling a friend about a dream he had, and the friend interpreted the dream to mean the Israelites would defeat them, Gideon's courage was renewed. He took the 300 men and split them up with trumpets, jars, and torches. Together, they made a huge ruckus, shouting, breaking the jars, and blowing the trumpets.

The Midianites were terrified. They fled, turning on each other with their swords.

The Israelites won the battle without even having to fight. That's what happens when God fights for you.

Verse to Remember - 2 Corinthians 12:9
Find this verse in your Bible and write it below.

____

____

____

____

Reflect - When we are following God, it's easy to feel alone and scared. The Bible makes it clear that following God won't be the popular choice. It can start to feel like Gideon with his 300 men against tens of thousands of people. But look what God did with those 300 men!

Trust God to do a lot with just a little. Trust Him to use you and work for you and through you, even when you feel like you're working against impossible odds. Write a prayer below and ask God to help you recognize your own weaknesses, but to trust His strength. Ask Him to help you remember to give Him credit for the amazing things He does.

Day 10: David & Goliath

David was chosen by God when he was just a young boy. The prophet Samuel anointed him as king when he was just ten to fifteen years old. Even Samuel was surprised by God's choice in this - David had older, stronger brothers, and on the outside, David was the least impressive of all his brothers. But he was the one God chose, and Samuel anointed David as the future king.

The Bible says the Spirit of the Lord "rushed upon David" at that time and stayed with him throughout all his days (1 Samuel 16:13). He didn't become king immediately, as King Saul was still in power, but it was his destiny to rule Israel someday. When Saul was suffering, he called for David to come and play music for him to help him feel better.

David was still a young boy when the Philistines gathered their armies to go to battle against Israel. They encamped on one side of the mountain, while the Israelites camped on the other, with a valley between them. Every day, one Philistine man came out of the camp to shout out a challenge to the Israelites. His name was Goliath, and he was a giant of around nine feet tall with armor and weapons to match his massive size. When he shouted his challenge, the Israelites trembled in fear. It looked like the Philistines would never be defeated.

BUT GOD.

David's older brothers were encamped with the Israelite army. David's father, Jesse, sent David to his brothers to bring them food and check on them. When David got there, he heard Goliath's challenge and saw the way the rest of the men cowered. "Who is this uncircumcised Philistine, that he should defy the armies of the living God?" David asked (1 Samuel 17:26). He focused on God's honor rather than Goliath's size.

David volunteered to fight Goliath. At first, Saul was against it, pointing out that David was just a boy while this man had been fighting in battle for years. But David knew God had been preparing him for this moment. He remembered the times he had struck down lions and bears on behalf of the sheep he protected. "The LORD who delivered me from the paw of the lion and from the paw of the bear will deliver me from the hand of this Philistine," David said with confidence (1 Samuel 17:37).

Saul tried to protect David, offering him armor and a sword. But David wasn't comfortable and refused Saul's help, instead taking five smooth stones and his sling. With that, he approached Goliath.

Goliath laughed and insulted David, cursing him by his gods. But David knew the battle was his. He told Goliath he may have fancy weapons and armor, but he had something bigger than that on his side: God. When Goliath arose and went to meet David, David didn't hesitate. He ran to the battle line to meet him, reaching into his bag and taking out a stone. He slung it and struck Goliath in the forehead, knocking him to the ground. David took Goliath's own sword and killed him with it. With God, the victory was David's.

Verse to Remember - 1 Samuel 17:45
Find this verse in your Bible and write it below.

____

____

____

____

Reflect - 1 Samuel 16:7 says, "For the LORD sees not as man sees: man looks on the outward appearance, but the LORD looks on the heart." Think about the characteristics we use to judge others. People look at outward appearance - looks, stature, social status. But God doesn't care about any of that. He sees right past it all, right to the heart. He looks at our character, our intentions, our motivations - things that aren't always visible to others.

Write a prayer to God below, asking Him to help you see others the way He does. Ask Him to help you look at what's inside a person instead of their outward appearance and characteristics. Ask Him to help you make your choices on who to surround yourself with based on those things instead of what the world tends to think is important.

____

____

____

____

____

____

____

____

Day 11: David & Saul

Naturally, after David killed Goliath, he gained quite the reputation. When he returned home, people came out from every city singing and dancing. They sang one song in particular that caused some problems: "Saul has struck down his thousands, and David his ten thousands" (1 Samuel 18:7). You can imagine the jealousy Saul felt when he heard this song. From that point on, he was filled with rage toward David.

While David was playing music, Saul hurled a spear at him, trying to kill him. David managed to evade him and continued to be successful in all he did. He even married Saul's daughter. Saul kept putting David in situations that he thought would put him in danger of death.

BUT GOD.

God was with David and he thrived. This is when Saul became more open with his desire to kill David. He told his son, Jonathan, and all his servants that they should kill him. But Jonathan and David were good friends, and Jonathan warned David of his father's plans. Jonathan managed to talk some sense into his father for a time, and Saul promised he wouldn't be put to death. But just a short time later, he tried once again to pin David to the wall with the spear. David escaped and fled from Saul that night.

At this point, Saul was determined to have David put to death.

BUT GOD.

Saul sent messengers looking for David, but again, God protected David. No one was able to bring David back to Saul. Jonathan made a plan to hide David and help him escape from Saul. David ended up living in a cave with a group of men who gathered to him. He became commander over them. Saul continued to pursue David, even murdering an entire family and a whole group of priests because one particular priest had helped David by giving him bread and a sword.

Saul took three thousand men with him in search of David. He entered a cave alone, not knowing that David and his men were sitting inside of it. David saw Saul, but Saul didn't see David.

This was his chance: he could kill Saul and end this life on the run once and for all.

BUT GOD.

David didn't have it in his heart to kill Saul. He didn't allow his men to do so, either. Instead, he cut off a corner of Saul's robe. He then went out of the cave after Saul, fell to the ground, and showed Saul the corner of his own robe. He explained that he had the chance to kill him and didn't take it. Saul was so moved that David had repaid his own evil with good that he admitted David would become the king and asked for mercy.

Of course, this peace only lasted a little while before Saul decided to attack David once again. He gathered thousands of men again and went out in pursuit of David.

BUT GOD.

David came upon Saul when he was in a deep sleep. Like before, he could have ended Saul's life then and there. But like before, he chose not to. He took the spear and the jar of water that lay beside Saul and crept away. He then called to Saul from afar and told him that once again, he had spared his life. Saul realized that he had sinned and promised to leave David in peace.

Eventually, Saul was murdered by Philistines and David became the new king, just as Samuel had anointed him to be all those years before. Saul was determined to take fate into his own hands to protect his position of power, but God's plans prevailed.

Verse to Remember - 1 Samuel 18:14
Find this verse in your Bible and write it below.

____

____

____

____

____

Reflect - Over and over again, David's life was in danger. He had thousands of men searching for him, seeking to kill him. Anyone would have been terrified. Anyone would have questioned God. It would have been easy to feel angry with Him, wondering why He allowed this to happen.

Read Psalm 56 in your Bible. David wrote this Psalm when he was running from Saul. Pay special attention to verses 3 and 4. Notice what David says he does when he feels afraid: he trusts in God.

Write a prayer below, asking God to help you keep your trust in Him when you feel afraid. Ask Him to help you have faith like David, knowing He is with you and protects you in all you do.

Day 12: Shadrach, Meshach, & Abednego

In another troubling time for the Israelites, King Nebuchadnezzar of Babylon conquered Jerusalem. He took many of God's people who lived there as captives, including Shadrach, Meshach, and Abednego. These three men were among the chosen in Babylon because they were bright, well-educated, and they impressed the king with their knowledge. They were taken to be trained in the culture and customs of Babylon and were even given new Babylonian names.

But then King Nebuchadnezzar made a huge image out of gold. He gathered all the people and told them that when they heard the sound of music, they had to fall down and worship the golden image. Anyone who refused to worship it would be cast into a fiery furnace.

This was a problem for Shadrach, Meshach, and Abednego. As children of God, they knew they could only worship one: the true God. So these brave men refused to fall down in worship like the rest of the Babylonian people. They heard the music, but they ignored it, even when others were around to watch them disobey the king's command.

Of course, the people ran straight to the king and told on Shadrach, Meshach, and Abednego. Nebuchadnezzar called them in and asked them point blank why they refused to worship his golden statue and reminded them of the punishment: the fiery furnace.

God's men stood their ground. They told the king that they believed God could save them from whatever punishment he might give them. But they also told him that even if He didn't - even if God chose NOT to save the lives of Shadrach, Meshach, and Abednego - they would still stand by him. Even if it meant death, they would follow Him.

Nebuchadnezzar was furious. He ordered the furnace to be heated seven times hotter than it usually was and prepared to throw Shadrach, Meshach, and Abednego in. He had them bound by strong men from his army, but the flames were so intense that some of those army men were killed by just approaching the furnace. And so Shadrach, Meshach, and Abednego fell into the burning fiery furnace to what should have been immediate death.

BUT GOD.

When King Nebuchadnezzar looked into the fire, he saw Shadrach, Meshach, and Abednego in there, walking around, unbound. But even more surprising was the appearance of a *fourth* man walking with them in that fire, whom King Nebuchadnezzar described as "a son of the gods" (Daniel 3:25).

Immediately, King Nebuchadnezzar called them from the fire. When they walked out, he found them perfectly fine - not even a hair singed. They didn't even smell like smoke!

Because of what Nebuchadnezzar witnessed, even he couldn't deny the power of God. He made a new decree: no one was allowed to speak anything against the God of Israel. He even promoted Shadrach, Meshach, and Abednego.

They took a huge risk. That furnace could have resulted in excruciating death. But God intervened, saving the lives of Shadrach, Meshach, and Abednego and showing his power to an entire nation. When it seemed hopeless, God showed up and did what only He can do - the impossible.

Verses to Remember - Daniel 3:17-18
Find these verses in your Bible and write them below.

____

____

____

____

Reflect - Shadrach, Meshach, and Abednego were confident in what God could do, but they were ready to follow Him to their deaths if they had to. Ask God to help you have a big faith like that: faith that follows Him no matter what the situation might be. Write a prayer below, asking God to help you have faith like these three incredible men.

____

____

____

____

____

____

____

____

Day 13: Daniel

Years after Shadrach, Meshach, and Abednego found themselves unharmed after walking through the fiery furnace, a man named Daniel found himself in a similar situation.

Like these three men, Daniel was an Israelite in Babylon. This time, the ruler was a man named King Darius. Just as Shadrach, Meshach, and Abednego found favor with Nebuchadnezzar, Daniel found favor with King Darius. He was a respected leader in the Babylonian court, serving King Darius well with much wisdom.

The other officials were jealous. They couldn't find anything wrong or illegal to pin on Daniel, so they came up with a plan: they would convince the king to decree that for a solid 30 days, no one could pray to any god except for him.

Daniel, who followed King Darius faithfully, knew he couldn't follow this rule. His faith in God was strong, and there was no way he was going to pray to anyone else.

Sure enough, the officials watched Daniel to catch him violating the law and praying to God. They couldn't get to King Darius fast enough to report Daniel. Darius was heartbroken because of his deep respect for Daniel, but he was bound by his own law. He had to give the order to throw Daniel into the den of hungry lions, knowing full well that Daniel would be devoured.

BUT GOD.

After a sleepless night where King Darius worried about Daniel, he ran to the den the next morning. Much to his shock, he found Daniel completely unharmed. Daniel explained to Darius that an angel shut the mouths of the lions, keeping him safe throughout the night.

Darius was filled with joy and had Daniel rescued from the lions' den. He acknowledged and celebrated the power of the God of Israel, even declaring that everyone in the kingdom would worship Him. He called in the officials who accused Daniel and threw them into the lions' den, and they were immediately devoured.

That lions' den was meant to be a death sentence, but God had other plans for Daniel. Daniel stood strong in his faith in God, refusing to worship anyone else, and God came through to use that faith to show the whole nation just who He really was. God's power and protection prevailed over evil in what seemed to be an impossible way.

Verse to Remember - Daniel 6:22
Find this verse in your Bible and write it below.

Reflect - This entire situation happened because of the jealousy of the other men who worked alongside Daniel in the court of Darius. Think about the lesson this story teaches us about the consequences of jealousy and deception.

In what areas of your life do you struggle with jealousy? Almost all of us struggle with this at some point in our lives - it's easy to feel jealous of others when they have more than we do, perform better than we do, or have something that we want.

Ask God to help you deal with those struggles. Write a prayer here asking God to show you where jealousy affects your life and to help you eliminate any jealousy you have toward others.

Day 14: Elijah & the Widow

Israel came to be ruled by a king named Ahab who was full of evil. He created an altar for Baal and led the people of Israel to worship this false god.

A prophet named Elijah warned Ahab that because of his actions, a drought would come upon the land. They would have no rain for years except by his word. He then went into hiding at God's command, where God promised to provide for him. Elijah lived alone in the wilderness, where God provided through a brook to drink and ravens who actually brought him bread and meat twice a day. Just as Elijah predicted, there was no rain, and eventually the brook he drank from dried up. Elijah had no water.

BUT GOD.

God spoke to Elijah and told him to go to a widow who would feed him. Elijah went where God told him to and found a widow gathering sticks. He asked her for some bread, but she said she had nothing more than a little flour in a jar and a little oil in a jug. She was gathering sticks to prepare a last meal for herself and her son, because after eating it, they would have nothing left and would die.

BUT GOD.

Elijah told her not to be afraid. He told her to make him a little cake from the supplies she had, and to prepare something for herself and her son as well. He promised her that her flour and oil would never run out until God sent rain to the earth again. The widow believed Elijah and did what he said, and just as he told her, her flour and oil never ran out. They were able to eat for many days on the little supplies she had.

However, the son of the widow became very sick. Eventually, he died. This boy was all she had, and he was gone. She was devastated and got upset with Elijah, feeling as if he caused the situation somehow.

BUT GOD.

Elijah took the boy and carried him to his bed. He cried out to God, then stretched himself over the boy three times, begging God to bring him back to life. God listened to Elijah's pleas and the boy lived! Elijah took the boy back down to his mother, who was filled with joy. She said to Elijah, "Now I know that you are a man of God, and that the word of the LORD in your mouth is truth" (1 Kings 17:24).

God provided for Elijah, the widow, and the boy in impossible ways. Thankfully, there is no *impossible* when it comes to God.

Verse to Remember - Luke 1:37
Find this verse in your Bible and write it below.

Reflect - Think about the way God provided for Elijah in the wilderness. He received his food each day from ravens! Imagine having birds that would bring you bread and meat twice a day. This shows that all of creation really does belong to God, that even the birds of the air listen to Him and obey His command.

Read Psalm 104 in your Bible. Write a prayer below, not asking God for anything today, but just praising Him as the Creator of everything. Praise Him for providing for you and for all of His creation. He is a good God and deserves our praise and thanks!

Day 15: Elijah & the Prophets of Baal

The drought went on for more than three years before God told Elijah to go back to Ahab, and He would send rain on the earth. The famine was severe at this point. Elijah met Obadiah, a man who feared God though he worked for King Ahab. When Jezebel, Ahab's wife, murdered God's prophets, Obadiah risked his life by hiding a hundred of them in a cave and feeding them. Obadiah told Elijah that Ahab had searched everywhere for him, blaming him for the drought upon the land. Elijah promised to show himself to Ahab that very day.

When Ahab finally saw Elijah, Elijah requested that the 450 prophets of Baal and the 400 prophets of Asherah who ate at Jezebel's table be brought to him. Ahab sent for them and gathered them together at Mount Carmel, where Elijah confronted them. He requested two bulls - one for himself and one for the false prophets. They would both lay their bulls on wood and call down fire; Elijah from God, and the false prophets from Baal.

The prophets of Baal went first. All morning, they cried and wailed and even cut themselves until they bled, begging Baal to send fire. No answer.

It was Elijah's turn. He built an altar, creating a trench around it and filling it with water. He covered the bull and the wood with water, too, making everything wet so it would be even harder - almost impossible - to burn.

BUT GOD.

He cried out to the Lord, asking Him to reveal Himself as the one true God in Israel so the people would know Him. And just like that, fire fell from heaven, consuming the bull, the wood, the stones, the dust, and even the water in the trench.

And just a little while after, the clouds grew black and a great rain fell upon the land for the first time in years.

Verse to Remember - 1 Kings 18:39
Find this verse in your Bible and write it below.

____

____

____

____

Reflect - In our culture, you don't hear much about people setting up altars and worshipping false gods like they did in Biblical times. However, this doesn't mean we don't worship other gods. Other gods include the things that get more of your love and attention than God. The things that take up attention in our hearts and minds over God. Common gods in our culture include money, sports, video games, power, popularity, and our appearance. While these aren't necessarily all "bad" things - for example, it isn't a bad thing to play or watch your favorite sports - it can become a god in your heart and mind when it becomes more important than God. Even good things can become gods or idols in our hearts, like our friendships, our family, or our education.

Search your heart, and be honest with yourself. What gods have you allowed to take center stage in your heart and mind? What in your life is getting more of your affection and attention than God? Write a prayer below, turning those things over to God and putting him back as Number One in your life. Ask Him to help you keep Him at the center of all you do, keeping the people and the hobbies that are important to you in the right perspective so that they don't become idols in your heart.

Day 16: Jonah

God came to Jonah with a job He needed him to do. He asked him to go to Nineveh, a Gentile city, and call them out on the evil they were doing. Jonah didn't want this job because a) He was afraid, and b) He didn't necessarily *want* them to escape judgment. After all, the people of Nineveh weren't Jewish. He didn't think they would listen to him and even if they did, he didn't believe they deserved a second chance to turn themselves around.

So, he went the opposite direction. He found a ship that was going to Tarshish, thinking he would run from God.

BUT GOD.

God knew Jonah as the one for the job. Obviously, there was nowhere Jonah could go that God couldn't see him. He sent a great wind upon the sea, causing a storm that almost destroyed the ship.

The sailors were terrified. They cried out to their own gods and threw cargo into the sea to try to lighten it. Jonah had gone down inside the ship and fell asleep, unaware of the chaos on deck. The captain came down and begged Jonah to come up and cry out to his god, as nothing they were doing seemed to be working.

The men got together and decided to cast lots to see who had caused the storm to come upon them. When the lot fell to Jonah, he wasn't surprised. He gave God the glory, saying, "I fear the LORD, the God of heaven, who made the sea and the dry land" (Jonah 1:9). The men were even more afraid and asked Jonah what they should do to make the storm calm. Jonah told them to pick him up and throw him into the sea, because he knew it was his fault for trying to flee from God. The men were hesitant, but when nothing else was working, they did what Jonah told them to do. The moment they threw him overboard, the storm calmed.

Jonah could have been left out there to die all alone at sea.

BUT GOD.

God sent a giant fish to swallow Jonah. There he lived for three days and three nights. While in the fish's belly, he prayed and repented of the sin of running away, giving thanks and praise to God. And God spoke to the fish, and the fish vomited Jonah right out onto dry land.

Again, God told Jonah to go to Nineveh. He didn't give up on him or try to send someone else to do the job He meant for Jonah. And this time, when

God asked, Jonah obeyed. When he preached to the people and warned them of God's judgment, the people believed him and repented of their sin. Because Jonah obeyed God, an entire city was saved from God's judgment.

Verse to Remember - Jonah 2:7
Find this verse in your Bible and write it below.

Reflect - One important thing to take away from this story is that God's mercy extends to everyone. He has mercy for you when you mess up, thankfully. But He also has mercy for the people who, by human standards, don't deserve it. The worst criminals. The cruelest people in school. His love and mercy extends to the people you consider your enemies, and we have to reflect that love and mercy, too.

Write a prayer below, asking God to help you embrace everyone in your path with mercy and compassion, even when they don't seem to deserve it. Ask Him to help you offer forgiveness and grace, just as God does for you.

Day 17: Esther

Esther was a young Jewish girl who found herself in a unique situation. The King of Persia, where Esther and other Jewish people lived after Babylon conquered Israel, found himself single and looking for a new wife. His former wife, Queen Vashti, was banished from the palace when she refused to come and show off for King Xerxes and his drunken friends at a huge banquet. To find a replacement wife, he called in all the young, eligible women and held a sort of "Miss Persian Empire" competition.

Beautiful Esther found favor with one of the king's servants, and he gave her advice to help her impress the king. She listened to his wisdom and it worked - Esther was chosen out of hundreds of women to become the new Queen of Persia! She had come quite a long way from being the child of Jewish exiles, raised in a foreign land. She didn't reveal her Jewish heritage to the king or anyone in the palace, as her cousin Mordecai advised her not to.

One day, when Mordecai was sitting at the king's gate, he overheard a plot to kill the king. He reported it to Esther, and when the situation was investigated and found to be true, the guilty men were hanged and Mordecai's role in reporting it was recorded in a book of chronicles in the king's presence.

Meanwhile, a man named Haman worked for the king. Haman was promoted above all the officials and expected everyone to bow down to him when he walked by. Mordecai, who only bowed to God, didn't bow to Haman when he passed by. This infuriated Haman to the point that he plotted against all the Jewish people. He convinced the king to proclaim a death sentence against them all.

Mordecai told Esther what had happened and asked for her help. Esther didn't know what she could do - after all, she wasn't even allowed to go see her own husband unless he called for her to do so. But Mordecai convinced her to help her people. She proclaimed a three-day fast to seek God's wisdom and help, then determined to approach the king.

Esther knew that if she went to the king without permission, he could banish her or even put her to death.

BUT GOD.

Esther planned a feast and invited the king, and to her relief, he agreed to come.

Meanwhile, Haman built a 75-foot-high gallows to use to hang Mordecai. The night before the feast, the king couldn't sleep and decided to read the book of chronicles. He came across the story of Mordecai, who reported the murder plot, and realized he had never rewarded Mordecai for his good deed. Ironically, Haman walked in just as the king was thinking about this, and the king asked for his help in deciding what could be done to honor someone. Haman, thinking the king just *had* to be talking about him, came up with a plan to give royal robes, a crown, and a horse to the person of honor. Imagine Haman's face at the moment when the king ordered Haman to give those things to Mordecai, the very one he was planning to murder!

When the king and Haman went to the feast with Queen Esther, she revealed her request: to save her people from the death sentence. She accused Haman of the plot to kill the Jews, and the king was furious. He sentenced Haman to death on the very gallows he had prepared for Mordecai.

The story of Esther shows that God can use you in even the strangest situations. When Esther was a young Jewish girl living in a foreign country, she likely never imagined she would one day be queen there. And she definitely never imagined she would be the one to save her people from death. But God put her in the right place at the right time, and because she followed Him and His plans, He used her to do something amazing.

Verse to Remember - Esther 4:14
Find this verse in your Bible and write it below.

____

____

____

____

Reflect - If you can take anything away from this story, it is that God has a purpose for your life. God brought Esther to a place and a situation that seemed difficult, but He used her there to save her entire race from annihilation. She had the courage to approach the king without being summoned, trusting that God would take care of her.

You may have times in your life when you find yourself wondering why you're in a particular place - in a difficult job, or surrounded by difficult people, or away from home and feeling lonely - and you may question why God has you there. Remember Esther, and know that God has a plan for you no matter where you are. Write a prayer below, asking God to help you seek His purpose in every situation He brings you through.

Day 18: Adam & Eve

Today's devotional is over the ultimate *But God* story. It's the story of Adam and Eve, the first two people ever created by God, and the complete and utter mess they made of His creation.

It may seem strange to talk about Adam and Eve now. This story came long before Noah, or Moses, or Daniel, or any of the others we've studied so far. But this story comes now because it serves as an introduction to the most important One in the Bible: Jesus.

Picture the Garden of Eden - the epitome of perfection. The world was new and pure. In the garden, there was no pain. No stress. No war or even death. God made a perfect garden and put Adam and Eve in charge of taking care of it. They were given only one rule: don't eat the fruit from ONE specific tree. Everything else in the garden was theirs.

Of course, being humans, they didn't listen. All it took was one conversation with Satan, who used one of his oldest tricks - he got them to focus on the one thing they *couldn't* have. Forget all the beauty and perfection around them. They decided to try that forbidden fruit, and just like that, sin entered the world.

Sin. The thing that separates us from God.

Like any good parent, God loves us and wants what's best for us. And being the Creator of literally everything, He knows what is best for us...which also means He knows what's *not* good for us.

He lays it all out for us - what we should and shouldn't do. And any time we disobey, whether it's a big thing or a tiny thing, it's sin.

And every single one of us is guilty.

The Bible tells us that the consequence for sin is death (Romans 6:23). It's a permanent separation from God.

BUT GOD.

God never wanted that separation. So He made a way for forgiveness.

In the Old Testament, the people followed a system of animal sacrifices. The idea was, they "transferred" their sin to an innocent animal who then died in their place. Because the reality is, death is the punishment for sin.

But the animal sacrifice system was never meant to be permanent. It merely pointed to a plan God had - a plan to send the ultimate sacrifice to die in our place.

Enter Jesus.

Jesus was fully God. He was there from the beginning, with God during creation. He was there when Adam and Eve made that fateful decision that changed the course of the whole world. And He left the beauty and wonder of Heaven to come here, knowing His sole purpose was to become fully human and die for us.

He knew He would live a perfect life, and yet people would accuse Him of things He didn't do. He knew He would perform miracles and point people to God, and the very ones who claimed to follow God would put Him on a cross to die.

But He came anyway.

And because of what He did on that cross…and because He rose and conquered death once and for all…we are forgiven.

All we have to do is believe in Jesus and what He did for us. We have to accept His gift - His free gift - and live our lives with Him as Lord. No more death, and no more animal sacrifices to take our sin from us; Jesus paid the price we owe once and for all.

We could never earn or deserve what Jesus did for us. But He loves us that much. When He hung on that cross that day, we were on His heart.

Through Jesus, God made a way for us. And because of what He did through the cross, we are no longer separated from God.

Verses to Remember: The Romans Road
You can use these verses in the book of Romans to understand the concept of salvation through Jesus, and to explain that concept to others. Write down the following verses.

Romans 3:23

____

____

____

____

Romans 6:23

Romans 5:8

Romans 10:9

Day 19: Jesus Turns Water into Wine

Jesus and His disciples were invited to a wedding feast, along with Jesus's mother, Mary. During the feast, they ran out of wine. This was a major social mistake for the groom's family, who provided the food and wine for the feast. To run out would ruin their reputation and bring shame for the new married couple. But buying more wasn't an option - it was much too expensive.

BUT GOD.

Mary knew where to go: God was right there, in human form. She went to Jesus for help, knowing He would have compassion for this family and could provide a solution for this problem. She instructed the servants to do whatever He told them to do.

There were six stone jars at the wedding feast, and each one held twenty to thirty gallons. Jesus told the servants to take the jars and fill them up with water. The servants were probably so confused. They must have wondered how this could possibly help the situation, but they listened. They filled the jars to the brim.

Next, Jesus told them to draw some out of the jar and take it to the master of the feast. They did it. When the master tasted this water, which was now wine, he was so impressed he actually called for the groom and thanked him for saving the "good wine" instead of serving it first.

This may seem like a strange miracle for Jesus to do in order to begin His ministry. After all, it didn't save anyone from sickness or danger. But it *did* save the family from embarrassment, a bad reputation, and draining their savings. It shows us that Jesus cares about the problems of His people and wants to help, no matter what those problems may be. He didn't use anything fancy or magic to bring about the miracle; He just used what they already had on hand. When the servants trusted and did what He said, not knowing what the results might be, He did something incredible. And when the people there saw what He could do, *they believed.*

Verse to Remember - John 2:11
Find this verse in your Bible and write it below.

____

____

____

Reflect - This story is important because it shows that Jesus cares about the details of our lives. What's important to us is important to Him, and He will intervene and do amazing things for us.

Sometimes, we don't ask Jesus to get involved in situations because in our eyes, they just don't seem like problems that are "big" enough to pray about. But Jesus wants to be part of your life - the big stuff AND the small stuff.

What "small" things are you holding back from talking to God about every day? Write a prayer here, asking God to be involved in even the little details. If you have specific things in mind that you haven't prayed about, here is your chance to get them out there.

Day 20: Jesus at the Pool of Bethesda

The Pool of Bethesda in Jerusalem was a pool of legend. It was believed that an angel came and stirred the waters of the pool, which brought healing to the first person who entered the water after it was stirred. Because of this legend, many blind, injured, and paralyzed people spent their time next to the waters, hoping to be the lucky one to reach the water first.

One man who lay there had been trying for *thirty-eight years* to reach those waters first. It seemed impossible; he had no one to help him get into the pool when the water was stirred up, and other people would beat him to the water every time. It seemed hopeless.

BUT GOD.

When Jesus appeared on the scene, he saw the man lying there. He asked the man if he wanted to be healed, and the man explained that it would never happen because he just wasn't fast enough on his own.

But Jesus had another plan for this man, and He didn't need the waters of the pool of Bethesda to heal him. He told the man, "Get up, take up your bed, and walk" (John 5:8).

Just get up and walk? That must have seemed like a ridiculous request. If the man could simply get up and walk away, he wouldn't have wasted all that time - all those years - lying by the water, hoping for a miracle.

BUT GOD.

When Jesus spoke, something happened. The man had the faith to do what Jesus asked him to do, and in that instant, he was better. He got up, picked up his mat, and walked away.

Of course, it just so happened to be the Sabbath day. The Jewish people had very strict ideas about what was allowed and not allowed on the Sabbath, the day of rest. When the religious leaders saw the man walking with his mat, they stopped him. It was considered "work" to carry the mat, and this wasn't allowed. But the man, overjoyed with his healing, told the religious leaders what Jesus had done for him.

For whatever reason, instead of being awed by the power of God, they were furious. Jesus dared to defy their man-made rules about the Sabbath by healing a man! They didn't care that He had done something amazing; they only cared that He didn't follow their rules.

But Jesus didn't worry about that. He knew He was there to share the love of God, and that meant healing those who were hurting. He continued on with His mission without fear of what the religious leaders would do about it. He knew it would eventually lead to the end of His time on earth, but that didn't matter to Him. The only thing that mattered was showing His people the deep, unconditional, amazing love and power of God.

Verses to Remember - John 5:8-9
Find these verses in your Bible and write them below.

____

____

____

____

Reflect - Jesus asked the man to get up and walk, knowing full well that for thirty-eight years, the man had been unable to do so. Yet, when Jesus asked him, he had enough faith to try. And look what happened! For the first time in what must have felt like forever, the man was strong and able to move by himself.

There will be times that Jesus may ask you to do something that seems too hard, maybe even impossible. You won't see Him standing in front of you or hear His voice out loud, but it's a small tug inside of you - an idea that just won't leave you - prompting you to do something. You may not see any way you could possibly do the thing that is weighing on your heart. This is where faith comes in! Trust that Jesus has a plan and will provide for you in whatever you need.

Now is the time to ask God to help you build that faith. Write a prayer here and ask Him to help you listen for His voice in your heart, and to have the faith to do whatever it is He asks of you.

____

____

____

____

____

____

Day 21: Jesus Heals the Leper

It's hard to think of a fate worse than leprosy during Biblical times. The disease started off with red spots that developed all over the skin, but got worse with time. Eventually, the victim would lose their hair and even their fingers and toes. Perhaps the worst part was the fact that as soon as you were diagnosed with it, you were on your own - no one else was allowed to be within six feet of you. Many Jewish people wouldn't even speak to one and would go out of their way to avoid any area where lepers existed. Not only was the victim sentenced to a slow, painful death...most people looked at him and felt pure disgust.

BUT GOD.

When Jesus was traveling around, preaching and sharing the Good News of the Kingdom of God, a man with leprosy had the nerve to approach him. This alone took a lot of faith on the part of the leper; many religious leaders bragged about their cruel treatment toward these poor people. But this man knew Jesus was different, and he gathered his courage and came to Him in desperation.

He got down on his knees and begged Jesus to make him clean.

When Jesus looked at this vulnerable, suffering man, He felt nothing but love and compassion. Then, He did something incredible: He reached out His hand and touched the man! He knew it had been such a long time since the man had felt a loving touch from anyone, so He chose the most loving way to heal this man.

And as soon as Jesus touched him, the leprosy was gone.

The man was ecstatic. He went out and told anyone in his path what Jesus had done for him. Because of his story, more and more people flocked to see this amazing miracle-worker. Jesus couldn't even enter a town without huge crowds of people gathering around to meet Him.

The leper's situation was hopeless. He had to watch himself deteriorate, knowing there was nothing he could do to be healed. He lost his family and friends. He was destined to live out his remaining days as a miserable, lonely man.

BUT GOD.

Verse to Remember - Matthew 8:3
Find this verse in your Bible and write it below.

Reflect - When the leper was healed, notice his response: he went out and told the world! His healing became an incredible testimony that brought many, many people to Jesus. When we know the love and incredible power of Jesus, we have to share it with others. This is the way to lead people to Him.

What is your testimony? Maybe you have a powerful story like the leper. Or maybe your story is simple, something much less "exciting." Either way, please know that there is no such thing as a bad testimony. God can use your story - whatever it might be - to impact others.

Spend some time thinking about this. How did you come to know Jesus? What has been His impact on your life so far? How have you changed since you began following Him? Write your testimony below and ask God to help you have the boldness to share your story with others.

Day 22: Jesus Heals the Paralyzed Man

The news of Jesus and His miracles spread like wildfire. When He came to speak, crowds were guaranteed to be there. When He arrived in Capernaum, many appeared at the house where He stayed to hear Him preach. So many people filled the house that soon, there was no more room for anyone else to come inside. Jesus taught the huge crowd about the Kingdom of God.

While He spoke, four men arrived at the house, carrying a paralyzed man on a bed. They were determined to get their friend to Jesus. They had heard of His miraculous healings. They knew if they could just get to Him, Jesus would heal their friend and he would walk again.

But the entrances were blocked. There was no room for even one man to squeeze inside, much less four men carrying another man on a bed. The situation looked hopeless.

BUT GOD.

The men knew they had to get creative. When they saw there was no way to get through the door, they climbed up to the roof of the house, carrying their friend along with them. This flat roof was made out of dried mud and clay. The men dug into the roof until they made a hole in it. When the hole was big enough, they started lowering their paralyzed friend, bed and all, into the home. Imagine what the crowds must have thought when they saw a man coming into the house above them!

When Jesus saw the faith of these men, He was filled with love and compassion for them. He looked at the paralyzed man and said, "Take heart, My son; your sins are forgiven" (Matthew 9:2). He knew that above anything else, this was the greatest pressing need of all humans: forgiveness. Forgiveness was more important than being able to walk again. Jesus is much more concerned with what is on the inside of a person than He is what's on the outside.

The Jewish leaders didn't like what Jesus said. In their minds, they complained. *Who does He think He is? No one can forgive sins but God alone.*

Though they didn't voice their complaints out loud, Jesus read their hearts. "Why do you think evil in your hearts?" He asked them. "For which is easier, to say, 'Your sins are forgiven,' or to say, 'Rise and walk'? But that you may know that the Son of Man has authority on earth to forgive sins...Rise, pick up your bed and go home" (Matthew 9:4-6).

The paralyzed man had never been able to get up on his own. He had never been able to pick up his own bed and walk.

BUT GOD.

When Jesus told him to do it, he let his faith be bigger than his doubt. And just like that, he stood up, picked up his bed, and walked out of the house.

All the people in the house witnessed this amazing moment and rejoiced. This man, who had accepted life as a paralytic, would never be the same again.

Verse to Remember - Mark 2:12
Find this verse in your Bible and write it below.

___

___

___

___

Reflect - This miracle never would have happened if the four men hadn't insisted on bringing their friend to Jesus. They didn't have to go to the trouble of carrying him to that house. When they saw the huge crowds, they could have easily given up and gone home. But they were determined to do whatever it took to get their friend to Him.

Think about your friendships. Are you surrounding yourself with friends who help you come to know Jesus? And maybe even more importantly, are you the kind of friend who helps others come to know Him?

Spend some time being honest with yourself. What kind of friend are you? What kind of friends do you choose? If you spend all your time with people who lead you in the opposite direction, you will find yourself slipping further and further away from Him.

Ask God to help you be like those four men who carried their friend to Jesus. Write a prayer and ask Him to help you go out of your way, out of your comfort zone, and insist on introducing your friends to Him. Ask Him to put friends in your life who will encourage you and lead you closer to Him along your path.

___

___

Day 23: Jesus Calms the Storm

After a full day of teaching the people, Jesus told the disciples it was time to move on to the next town. They got into a boat and started across the water of the Sea of Galilee, leaving the crowd of people.

Suddenly, a great windstorm came up. The waves rose so high they began breaking into the boat, filling it with water. The disciples were afraid for their lives.

BUT GOD.

The disciples remembered Who they had in the boat with them. They went to Jesus, hoping He could help…and they found Him asleep! While they were in a panic, He slept soundly on the cushion in the stern of the boat.

Jesus was tired. Yes, He was fully God, but He was also fully human. The demands of the constant teaching and traveling wore Him down until He was able to sleep through the violent storm.

But it wasn't just exhaustion that let Him sleep in that storm. Jesus knew God. He knew God would protect Him, no matter how bad the storm got. Worry wouldn't keep Him awake. His trust allowed Him to rest, even when it seemed as if death surrounded them in that boat.

The disciples didn't understand all that. When they found Jesus asleep, their panic grew. They were on the verge of death, and Jesus wasn't helping. "Teacher, do you not care that we are perishing?" they asked in desperation, waking Him from His sleep.

BUT GOD.

Jesus simply looked around at the violent storm and spoke to the wind, commanding it to stop. He said to the sea, "Peace! Be still!" (Mark 4:39).

The moment He simply spoke, the wind stopped blowing and the sea became calm.

The disciples were amazed to the point of fear. They didn't understand how even the wind and waves obeyed Jesus. Even though they had seen Him do miracle after miracle, watching Him control nature was a whole new level of incredible.

They knew God could control the elements. Watching Jesus command them with the same authority as God helped them start to fully understand just Who He really was.

Verse to Remember - Mark 4:39
Find this verse in your Bible and write it below.

Reflect - When you truly remember just how big our God is, everything else will seem so small. If you picture the God who created everything - the oceans, the mountains, the forests, and the sunsets - that "big problem" in your life will shrink. If God is by your side, what do you have to fear? If God is in control during even the scariest situations, doesn't that bring you comfort and peace in the midst of them?

At this moment, don't ask God for anything. Take another chance to just offer Him praise. Write a prayer below, praising Him for Who He is. Recognize Him as the Creator of all things, including you, and thank Him for having a good plan for your life. Give Him the praise and thanks that He deserves for all He is and all He does.

Day 24: The Woman Who Touched His Garment

A woman had a condition that made her bleed for twelve years. Take a moment to imagine what that would be like. Twelve years?! She had spent all her money seeing doctors, searching for healing, but nothing worked. Instead of getting better, she got worse. Because she was bleeding, she was considered "unclean" and was treated like an outcast. She lost her friends and even her family because of her condition.

BUT GOD.

The woman heard about Jesus and was desperate to get to Him. She knew He was her only hope. And one day, she finally had her chance to see Him.

The problem was, Jesus was flocked by the crowds. Everyone had heard about Jesus and what He could do, so they followed Him closely, sticking by His side. The woman took one look at the crowd and knew she had no chance of getting any one-on-one time with Him. She could have given up right then and there.

BUT GOD.

Her faith in Jesus and what He could do carried her to do something extreme. She pushed her way through the crowd, approaching Jesus from behind. Her goal wasn't to ask Him to heal her or to even talk to Him at all; she simply wanted to touch His garment. Her faith was so strong that she believed if she just touched something He wore, she would be healed.

Finally, the moment came that she could reach out and touch His garment. She likely thought she could accomplish this without Him even noticing - with such a huge crowd surrounding Him closely, He had to have been touched constantly. Just as she suspected, as soon as she touched Him, she was healed!

But Jesus felt the power that left Him the second the woman reached out to Him. He stopped right in the middle of what He was doing and spoke to the crowd, asking who touched Him.

The disciples must have thought He was crazy. How could He ask who had touched Him when people pressed in all around Him? But Jesus knew something had happened. It wasn't that He had a "magical" garment; if that was true, everyone in the crowd would have been healed from whatever ailments they had. The power was in Him, and in the faith of the woman. Because she believed, she was healed.

The woman was terrified as she came forward to confess. Trembling, she fell at His feet and confessed her story - how she had been sick for so long, and He was her only hope. She must have thought Jesus would be angry with her for sneaking up on Him and "stealing" His power.

BUT GOD.

Jesus loved her. He knew exactly who she was, and He knew her story before she ever told it. He wanted her to come to Him, to let Him speak to her and assure her of His love. She didn't have to "steal" that power; He gave it to her willingly.

Jesus may not walk among us in this world today, but His power is still here. It lives in everyone who believes in Him and makes Him the Lord of his or her life. It just takes faith like the woman who reached out to touch His garment.

Verse to Remember - Matthew 9:22
Find this verse in your Bible and write it below.

____

____

____

____

Reflect - Because of her bleeding condition, society was repulsed by this woman. They went out of their way to avoid touching her. But Jesus didn't respond with disgust. He responded with peace, acceptance, and grace. He called her His daughter and offered her healing.

Think about your own life for a moment. Have you ever felt like an outcast? Have you ever felt abandoned? Take comfort in knowing that Jesus loves you and will never abandon you. Now, think about others you know who are considered outcasts. The kids at school who have trouble making and keeping friends. How does Jesus feel about those people? And if you know that Jesus loves them, what does that say about how you should treat them?

Write a prayer below, asking God to help you reach out to Him when you feel alone. Ask Him to help you show His love to those around you who may be treated like outcasts.

____

____

Day 25: Jesus Brings the Girl Back to Life

There's more to the story in the last devotional, the one where Jesus healed the woman who had been bleeding for twelve years. Something happened right before and right after His encounter with that woman, and that's where today's focus will be.

Before Jesus walked with the crowd and the woman reached out to touch His garment, a man approached Jesus in desperation. The man's name was Jairus, and he was one of the religious leaders. Jairus's twelve-year-old daughter was very sick, almost to the point of death. He needed a miracle.

He had heard about Jesus. He came to Him and begged Him to lay His hands on his little girl, making her well again. Jesus had compassion for Jairus and the little girl and agreed to go with him to see the little girl.

Meanwhile, as they walked to Jairus's house in the midst of the crowd, the woman approached Jesus and caused a commotion that slowed Him down. As soon as He told the woman to go in peace because her faith had made her well, a man came running to Jairus with some terrible news. He told Jairus that his daughter was dead and he shouldn't trouble Jesus any longer. It was too late. They hadn't made it to her in time, and now she was gone.

BUT GOD.

Jesus overheard the conversation, but he wasn't shaken up by the news. He told Jairus not to be afraid, but to believe.

Jesus and Jairus left the crowd behind, taking only a few of the disciples with them as they went to Jairus's house. At the home, people wept and wailed loudly for the little girl. Jesus asked the mourners to leave. "Go away, for the girl is not dead but sleeping" (Matthew 9:24). The mourners laughed at Him. They knew the little girl was dead.

BUT GOD.

When the crowd was outside, Jesus went in to see the little girl. He took her by the hand and told her to get up…and she did. She walked and talked as if she had never even been sick, much less dead.

Even death wasn't a match for God.

Verse to Remember - Matthew 9:25
Find this verse in your Bible and write it below.

Reflect - Sometimes our timing and God's timing don't line up the way we think it should. We often want things done immediately, and we expect God to answer our prayers that way as well. One thing this story shows is that even when it seemed as if Jesus was "too late," the truth is, God isn't bound by time like we are. If God wants to make something happen, it will happen, in His own perfect timing.

One of the most difficult things in the Christian life is waiting for an answer to a prayer. Maybe you've been praying about something and haven't seen the answer yet. Write a prayer here, asking God to help you to trust His timing in your life. Tell Him you know nothing is impossible with Him, and that you have faith that He will answer in His own perfect way.

Day 26: Jesus Feeds the 5,000

Over time, it became impossible for Jesus to go anywhere without massive crowds following Him. With every miracle He performed, His reputation spread further across the region. But Jesus, who was fully God, was also fully human, and even He needed rest at times. And after His disciples returned from a trip where they had preached and healed in the name of Jesus, they were exhausted, too. Jesus knew they all needed some time to rest and recover. He took them out in a boat and they went away to a quiet place by themselves.

But it was too late. People had already seen them and knew who they were. They figured out where Jesus and His disciples were going, and they came from towns all around, running ahead on foot to wait for them to arrive.

When they arrived on shore, there were 5,000 men waiting for them. Including the women and children, there were likely 15,000 people or more. So much for His plan to get away and rest for a while! But Jesus wasn't irritated. Instead, He was filled with compassion. He saw their needs and their hurts, and He loved them. Immediately, He began to teach them and heal their sick.

When it grew late, the disciples started to worry. The people would need to eat, and in the desolate place where they were, there would never be enough food for nearly 20,000 people. They asked Jesus to send the people away into the neighboring towns to find food.

But Jesus had other plans. He instructed His disciples to give the people something to eat.

The disciples were confused. How in the world would they be able to feed this crowd? It was impossible! They had no food and no money. It would take an entire year's income to feed them all.

BUT GOD.

They should have known by this point - with Jesus, there's always a way. "How many loaves do you have? Go and see," He instructed the disciples (Mark 6:38).

The disciples were able to find one young boy who had five loaves of bread and two fish. It wouldn't have gotten them very far.

BUT GOD.

Jesus had the people sit down in groups. He gave thanks to God and started passing out the food. The people ate as much as they wanted until they were full, and even then, the disciples managed to pick up *twelve baskets* of leftovers!

Jesus provided a way when the disciples couldn't see a way. He used what little they had available and turned it into something amazing. You can trust that He will always provide for you, even when your situation looks impossible. Just be willing to trust Him with what you have, even if it seems like very little.

Verse to Remember - Mark 6:42
Find this verse in your Bible and write it below.

____

____

____

____

Reflect - Sometimes it's easy to think that just because you're young, you can't do much for God. But the young boy in this story was willing to give Jesus what little he had, and look what He was able to do with it!

Write a prayer to God, asking Him to use you and what you have to do His will. Tell Him you're willing to give it all to Him, trusting Him to do amazing things through it.

____

____

____

____

____

____

____

____

Day 27: Jesus Heals the Blind

Imagine experiencing the world around you without sight. Think about the challenges and adaptations you would have to make - simple, everyday things you take for granted would require assistance. Things like reading. Cooking. Navigating your way through rooms and down hallways.

Some people are born blind. Others become blind over time due to injuries, age, or disease. In Biblical times, blindness was incurable. Even in today's world, there isn't a universal cure for all the different types of blindness.

BUT GOD.

The gospels share multiple instances where Jesus was able to heal the blind.

One instance was when Jesus and His disciples traveled to a town called Bethsaida. Some people there brought a blind man to Jesus and begged Him to touch and heal the man. Jesus took the blind man by the hand and led him out of the village. He spat on the man's eyes and laid His hands on him and asked him if he saw anything.

The man looked around. "I see people, but they look like trees, walking," he said (Mark 8:24).

Jesus laid His hands on the man's eyes again. This time, when he opened his eyes, he could see everything clearly.

In another situation, Jesus and His disciples saw a man blind from birth. The disciples began to ask Jesus questions, wondering if the man was blind because of sin in his life or in the life of his family. Jesus told them it was neither of those things; He would use the man's blindness to show the power of God. With that, He spat on the ground and made mud with His saliva. He rubbed the mud over the man's eyes and instructed him to go wash in the Pool of Siloam. When the man followed the orders of Jesus, he came back able to see.

Both of these stories show that sometimes God heals in really unconventional ways. We may never know why God chose to use spit and mud to heal blindness, but the truth is, it doesn't matter. God's ways are higher than ours, and while we won't always understand His methods, we can trust that He is working for our good.

Maybe someday your miracle will come through something really unexpected.

Verse to Remember - John 9:11

Find this verse in your Bible and write it below.

Reflect - Although you may not be physically blind, you may be blind spiritually at times. It's easy to get wrapped up in our busy schedules and even our sin and "close our eyes" to what God is doing all around us.

Jesus is able to open our eyes to Him, just as He opened the eyes of the blind men in the Bible. Write a prayer to Him, asking Him to open your eyes to what He is doing in your life. Ask Him to help you see His hand in everything, especially the unexpected.

Day 28: Jesus Heals the Bent Woman

One Sabbath day, Jesus was teaching in the synagogues. During Biblical times, men and women were welcome in the synagogues, although men were generally in the front of the audience while the women were put behind them. One particular woman was there that day. The Bible doesn't tell us her name or anything about her background, other than the fact that she had something wrong that made her bend over to where she couldn't straighten up.

We don't know what caused the condition. Maybe it was an injury. Maybe she had some sort of spinal disorder. Whatever it was, put yourself in her position. Imagine what it was like to walk around all day without being able to straighten your back. Looking down at the floor all the time, unable to make eye contact with others.

It's likely this woman accepted this condition as something she was stuck with. The condition was incurable, and she had no choice but to live with it.

BUT GOD.

While others may not have noticed this woman, Jesus did.

Jesus looked past the men and saw this woman among all the other women. And even though she couldn't look up to see Him, He was filled with compassion for her. He called her out of the crowd and told her she was free of her disability. He laid His hands on her, and just like that, she stood up straight. The first thing she did with her new freedom was give glory and thanks to God.

This was a miracle! But, as usual, the Pharisees weren't happy. First of all, Jesus healed on the Sabbath again - and they made a rule that you couldn't "do any work" on the Sabbath. Second, Jesus put His hands on this woman to heal her. In Biblical culture, a man wasn't supposed to touch a woman who was a stranger...especially not in public. So instead of recognizing the miracle of what Jesus did and being happy for the woman who was free from her condition, they got caught up in the man-made rules Jesus broke.

They called Jesus out on what He had done. But instead of apologizing for breaking their rules, Jesus pointed out the hypocrisy of the situation: they took care of their animals on the Sabbath, but He wasn't allowed to take care of His people?

You can imagine how the religious leaders felt when Jesus put them in their place. The more angry the Pharisees got, the more they wanted to get

Jesus out of the picture. It wouldn't be long before they would make a plan to put Him on trial and sentence Him to death.

And even then, there's a BUT GOD.

But that's a topic we'll get to in a future devotion.

Verse to Remember - Luke 13:13
Find this verse in your Bible and write it below.

____

____

____

____

Reflect - Imagine what the woman must have felt when Jesus laid His hands on her and she realized she could stand up. Imagine what it must have been like to look someone in the face for the first time in years. What was her response? She immediately gave God the glory.

Sometimes, when something good or even amazing happens in our lives, we forget to give God the thanks and praise He deserves. Think about your life. What has God done for you that deserves your praise? Write a prayer here, thanking God for the good things He has done for you.

____

____

____

____

____

____

____

____

Day 29: Jesus Raises Lazarus From the Grave

In the village of Bethany, a man named Lazarus was sick. Lazarus happened to be a good friend of Jesus. He was close with the family of Lazarus, including his sisters, Mary and Martha. Jesus knew this family well and had spent time with them. He loved them. So when Lazarus became sick, Mary and Martha sent word to Jesus.

When Jesus heard the news, He announced to His disciples that the illness would not lead to death. He knew He was going to go to Lazarus to heal him, but He didn't hurry. He stayed where He was for two more days before He told His disciples they must go to Lazarus. He told them Lazarus had fallen asleep and He was on His way to wake him up.

The disciples were confused. So Jesus explained what He meant: Lazarus had died. But He knew He was about to do something incredible.

By the time Jesus and His disciples got to Bethany, Lazarus had already been in the tomb for four days. Many people were at the home of Mary and Martha, comforting them.

Martha heard Jesus was coming, and she went out to meet Him. "Lord, if You had been here, my brother would not have died," she said. "But even now I know that whatever You ask from God, God will give You" (John 11:21-22).

But Jesus had good news for Martha. "Your brother will rise again…I am the resurrection and the life. Whoever believes in Me, though he die, yet shall he live" (John 11:23-25).

Mary and Martha took Jesus to the tomb. When He got there, He wept. He knew the miracle He was about to perform, and yet He wept for the loss of His friend and the pain His family and friends were feeling. They were still overwhelmed by the loss of someone they all loved so much.

BUT GOD.

Jesus ordered the stone be removed from the tomb, but Martha hesitated. She knew after four days, the body would begin to smell. But Jesus insisted, telling her to believe. He cried out with a loud voice, "Lazarus, come out" (John 11:43).

And with that, Lazarus walked out of the tomb! His hands and feet were still bound with the linen strips they had used for burial, and his face was still wrapped with a cloth. Jesus said to unbind him and let him go.

Soon, everyone was talking about the amazing thing Jesus had done. If the Pharisees were angry before, now they were furious. They didn't like the attention Jesus was getting or the fact that people were starting to believe in Him.

The plan to get Jesus out of the picture was starting to form in more detail.

Verses to Remember - John 11:25-26
Find these verses in your Bible and write them below.

____

____

____

____

Reflect - This story shows that Jesus has complete power over death. While we know that death is inevitable, we also know that through Jesus, death isn't the end.

Jesus can bring new life into anything. When it looks like the end, when the facts say that it's over, Jesus can do the impossible.

After four days of Lazarus being in the tomb, Mary and Martha never dreamed there was still a chance they would see their brother again in this life. But once again, God's timing wasn't their timing, and His timing was perfect.

Do you have a situation in your life that needs Jesus? Write a prayer here, asking Him to bring new life into it. Maybe you don't have a situation like that personally, but you likely know someone who does. Ask Jesus to do the impossible and bring a miracle that will help everyone see His mighty power.

____

____

____

____

____

____

____

Day 30: The Death & Resurrection

Jesus knew what the Pharisees were plotting. In fact, He warned His disciples multiple times that He would suffer and be rejected. He told them He would be mocked and beaten. Though His warning was scary, He knew death wouldn't be the end for Him. He knew three days later, He would rise from the dead.

The disciples didn't really understand. How could their Savior be put to death? How could this man who had performed miracle after miracle be beaten and mocked?

But just as Jesus predicted, it happened.

A week before His death, He rode into Jerusalem on a donkey while people shouted praises to Him. But behind the scenes, the plan to put Him to death was already underway. Judas, one of His own disciples, gave Him up to the Pharisees for thirty pieces of silver. The night before His death, He gathered with His disciples - even Judas - to celebrate the Passover. He knew He was living in His final hours, and yet what did He do? He washed the feet of His disciples and shared a meal with them. He warned them gently that they would betray Him that night, abandoning Him when He was put on trial. The disciples denied it, claiming they would never abandon their Messiah. But Jesus could see into the future, and He knew they would do just what He said. His love is that powerful, that unconditional. He was willing to go to the cross and die for them, even when they wouldn't be strong enough to stay by His side in His worst moments.

Everything Jesus told them would happen came true. That very night, He was arrested and put on trial. He was sentenced to death, even though they couldn't find anything that He had done wrong. And the disciples fled from the scene, with Peter even denying He ever knew Jesus.

Jesus was beaten with a whip full of spikes. He endured horrible pain and blood loss while the people placed a crown of thorns on His head, mocking Him and hurling insults at Him. And when He was weakened almost to the point of death, they nailed Him to the wooden cross to watch Him die.

BUT GOD.

Even as He hung dying on that cross, He still loved humanity. "Father, forgive them, for they know not what they do," He cried out (Luke 23:34).

Unexplained darkness covered the land for three hours while Jesus hung there until finally, He took His last breath. Suddenly, the earth shook. The rocks were split. The curtain of the temple was torn in two. Graves opened and bodies came out. Even the Roman guards who witnessed it all knew that this had to be the Son of God.

The Pharisees ordered a guard to make Jesus's tomb as secure as possible. They knew that Jesus had said He would rise again, and they were determined to make sure that didn't happen.

BUT GOD.

When some of His followers came to the tomb on the third day to prepare His body with spices, they found quite a shock: the body of Jesus wasn't there. The stone was rolled away and an angel sat on top of it, telling them that Jesus had risen just as He said He would! The soldiers who had been there to guard the tomb had become frozen with fear.

For forty days after His resurrection, He appeared to His disciples and many other eyewitnesses. Finally, He ascended into heaven, telling His disciples to share Him with the whole world.

Because Jesus conquered death, it has no power over us, either! When we make Him the Lord of our lives, we will spend our eternity with Him in heaven.

Verses to Remember - Matthew 28:19-20
Find these verses in your Bible and write them below.

____

____

____

____

Reflect - The verses you wrote above are known as "The Great Commission." These were Jesus's final words to His disciples, and they are for us, too. Our job as Christians is to share Jesus with the world. We can share His love and what it means to follow Him.

That's not always easy. We live in a world that doesn't want to hear about Jesus, but needs Him desperately. Write a prayer asking God to help you with this huge task. Ask Him to give you the words to say and the opportunities to talk about Jesus with the people in your path.

Bible Verse Memorization Challenge

There's this moment in the Bible when Jesus is out in the wilderness, alone with Satan. Over and over again, Satan tempted Him, trying His best to get Him to sin and ruin God's perfect plan for humanity. But over and over again, Jesus resisted temptation and triumphed over Satan.

The only weapon Jesus used against Satan was Scripture. When Satan dangled something in front of His face, Jesus refused it, citing the Word of God.

If Jesus used the Bible to fight against Satan, we should, too. Memorizing Scripture is one of the most effective ways to stay strong in the face of temptation.

Here are some good verses to tuck in your heart and mind to help you remember how good God is and how He works in your life. Write them below and spend some time each day reading over them. Challenge yourself to memorize them, focusing on just one at a time until you know them all.

Verse #1: 1 Peter 5:7

____

____

____

Verse #2: Romans 8:28

____

____

____

Verse #3: Romans 12:2

____

____

____

Verse #4: Isaiah 41:10

____

____

Verse #5: Matthew 11:28-30

Verse #6: 1 Thessalonians 5:16-18

Verse #7: Proverbs 3:5-6

Verse #8: Philippians 4:13

Verse #9: Psalms 56:3

Verse #10: Matthew 5:16

Verse #11: ______________________________ (Your choice)

____

____

____

Verse #12: ______________________________ (Your choice)

____

____

____

Verse #13: ______________________________ (Your choice)

____

____

____

Verse #14: ______________________________ (Your choice)

____

____

____

Verse #15: ______________________________ (Your choice)

____

____

____

30 Days of Gratitude Challenge

The Bible reminds us over and over again to be thankful. God knew what He was doing when He encouraged gratitude: studies show that being thankful has some really amazing mental and physical benefits. It promotes happiness and a good mood, reduces stress and anxiety, and improves your relationships with others. It can even improve your sleep and lower your risk for heart disease, which could help you live longer!

God is so good, and He puts blessings in your path every day. The more you take the time to notice those blessings and thank Him for it, the happier and healthier you will be.

This challenge will help you focus on the goodness of God in your life. It is so easy to focus on the negative: our shortcomings, our heartaches, and the bad situations we face. But the truth is, no matter what your life is like and no matter what you may be going through in this season of life, there is *always* something to be thankful for. God is working in your life in ways you may not even notice if you don't take the time to look for them.

For the next thirty days, your challenge is to find something good in your life every single day - big or small - and write it down here. It may be some really big, exciting moment, or it may be something as simple as a warm bed to sleep in. Whatever God shows you that day, write it down. When you write your blessing each day, be sure to thank God for it. Feel free to write more than one thing each day!

Day 1:

____

____

____

Day 2:

____

____

____

Day 3:

____

Day 4:

Day 5:

Day 6:

Day 7:

Day 8:

Day 9:

Day 10:

Day 11:

Day 12:

Day 13:

Day 14:

Day 15:

Day 16:

Day 17:

Day 18:

Day 19:

Day 20:

Day 21:

Day 22:

Day 23:

Day 24:

Day 25:

Day 26:

Day 27:

Day 28:

Day 29:

Day 30:

About the Author

Katy Newton Naas spends much of her free time chasing her two young boys, three dogs, five cats, and eight ducks. She has published more than forty children's, young adult, and adult books, including YA Christian Book of the Year Award-winning novel, *Healing Rain*, and Literary Classics International Book Gold Award-winning novel, *Guardian*. She enjoys serving as youth leader in her church and teaching middle school reading and language arts in the local school system. Find her books at:

https://www.etsy.com/shop/BooksbyKNN.

Made in USA - Kendallville, IN
68903_9798985846898
10.15.2025 2126